A Crabtree Branches Book

Catch the Wave

KITESURFING

Kerri Mazzarella

Crabtree Publishing
crabtreebooks.com

School-to-Home Support for Caregivers and Teachers

This high-interest book is designed to motivate striving students with engaging topics while building fluency, vocabulary, and an interest in reading. Here are a few questions and activities to help the reader build upon his or her comprehension skills.

Before Reading:

- *What do I think this book is about?*
- *What do I know about this topic?*
- *What do I want to learn about this topic?*
- *Why am I reading this book?*

During Reading:

- *I wonder why...*
- *I'm curious to know...*
- *How is this like something I already know?*
- *What have I learned so far?*

After Reading:

- *What was the author trying to teach me?*
- *What are some details?*
- *How did the photographs and captions help me understand more?*
- *Read the book again and look for the vocabulary words.*
- *What questions do I still have?*

Extension Activities:

- *What was your favorite part of the book? Write a paragraph on it.*
- *Draw a picture of your favorite thing you learned from the book.*

Table of Contents

WHAT IS KITESURFING?

Kitesurfing is a type of surfing that uses wind as power. It is just one of the many types of surfing you can try. A special board and **kite** are used by the surfer to glide across the water.

Fact

Kitesurfing is also known as kiteboarding.

Kitesurfing is a **watersport** practiced all over the world by many adventurous people. All you need is some water and wind!

Kitesurfing is considered an **extreme sport**. If the wind is strong, a surfer can be launched several feet (meters) up in the air.

The sport of kitesurfing, as we know it today, began in the 1990s. But the idea of kitesurfing may have started in the 1970s.

Fact

In 1984, French brothers Bruno and Dominique Legaignoux designed the first inflatable kite for kitesurfing. This design was improved over time and is still used today.

WHO CAN KITESURF?

Anyone can learn to kitesurf. It takes hard work and practice to get the hang of it.

Fact

A kiteboarding instructor will cost $50 to $150 per hour.

Kitesurfing can be challenging to learn at first. It is important to find a qualified, or trained, **instructor**. You can expect to take around 10 hours of lessons to start.

Hand-eye coordination and **balance** are great skills for kitesurfing. It is important to keep calm under pressure and be patient with yourself while learning.

CHOOSING YOUR EQUIPMENT

Equipment is a very important part of kitesurfing. First, you will need a kite to capture the wind and get you moving! There are many different shapes and sizes to choose from.

Next, you will need a kitesurfing board. The most common board is called a twin tip. Some kitesurfers also use directional or hydrofoil boards.

hydrofoil board

directional board

twin tip board

Fact

The cost of a basic kitesurfing kit that includes everything you need will range from $1,500 to $5,000.

The **control bar**, lines, and **harness** are also very important pieces of kitesurfing equipment.

WHERE TO KITESURF

Kitesurfing is practiced all over the world. Lakes, lagoons, bays, rivers, and oceans are all great places to kitesurf.

Fact

Some of the most popular kitesurfing destinations in the world include Maui, Hawaii; Cabarete, Dominican Republic; Cape Town, South Africa; and Tarifa, Spain.

For beginners, it is important to choose a large body of water that is wide open. It should be clear of anything that would get in the way of your kite.

There are plenty of places to choose from to begin your kitesurfing adventure. All you need now is some wind.

HOW TO KITESURF

As a beginner kitesurfer, you should take lessons from an experienced instructor. They will teach you the basics and how to use your equipment safely.

Your first lesson will include how to set up, carry, and control your kite on land. The instructor will go over hand positions on the bar and how to steer your kite.

Once you understand the basics and can control your kite, you will be ready to try kitesurfing! It will be best to stay in shallow water at first.

Fact

Kitesurfers must learn about wind direction and how it helps the kite fly. Downwind means moving with the wind behind the kite. Upwind means moving toward or against the wind.

Your kitesurfing instructor will help you learn how to launch the kite in the water and use the wind as power. You will learn how to use your body to control your movement.

FOR YOUR SAFETY

Safety is the most important thing when it comes to kitesurfing. You must have equipment that fits you properly, such as a helmet and a life jacket. If the water is cold, wear a **wetsuit** to keep warm.

A chicken loop acts as a break system for your kite. When it is pulled, it makes your kite lose power and stop.

Fact

The chicken loop is hooked to your harness.

To stay safe, kitesurfers also use a kite **leash**, avoid bad weather, and use the buddy system. They also keep their distance from others in the water.

FAMOUS KITESURFERS

Kitesurfing has become more popular in the last 20 years. In 2024, it was recognized as a sport in the Olympics.

Ellie Aldridge

Fact

The 2024 Paris Olympics featured kitesurfing for the first time. Ellie Aldridge of Great Britain won the gold medal for women and Valentin Bontus of Austria won the gold medal for men.

Fact

Each year, Red Bull sponsors the King of the Air competition for the best kitesurfers in the world. It takes place at Kite Beach in Cape Town, South Africa.

Some famous kitesurfers include Robby Naish, Susi Mai, and Aaron Hadlow. They have all helped to expand the sport of kitesurfing.

Susi Mai

RESPECTING OUR OCEANS

It is very important to respect our oceans. They provide many important benefits to people and all living things.

Fact

The ocean covers more than two thirds of Earth's surface.

The ocean provides more than half the oxygen we breathe. We can respect it by doing our part to keep it clean.

Fact

You can keep the ocean clean by picking up trash, even if it is not yours. You can also use ocean-safe products such as sunscreen.

Part of respecting the ocean as a kitesurfer is knowing your limits. The ocean is a beautiful place, but it is powerful and can be dangerous.

Kitesurfing is a fun sport and a great way to push your limits both physically and mentally. If you like a good thrill, get out there and give it a try!

Glossary

balance (bal-uhns): Your ability to remain steady and upright

control bar (kuhn-trohl bahr): A solid metal or composite bar that is used to steer and control the kite

equipment (i-kwip-muhnt): The tools or products needed for a particular purpose

extreme sport (ik-streem sport): Activities or sports that involve a high risk of injury and a thrilling feeling of excitement

harness (hahr-nis): A set of straps used to connect you to something to keep you safe

instructor (in-struhkt-ur): A person who teaches a subject or skill

kite (kite): A light frame covered with material that is attached to a long line and flown in the wind

leash (leesh): A strap or cord that is used to stay connected to your kite when you hit the safety release

watersport (waw-tur-sport): Sports that are carried out on or in water

wetsuit (wet-soot): A close-fitting suit, usually made of a type of rubber called neoprene, that is worn in cold water to retain body heat

Index

Websites to Visit

https://kids.kiddle.co/Surfing

https://www.surfertoday.com/kiteboarding/what-is-kiteboarding#google_vignette

https://elitewatersports.com/blogs/beginner-information/the-history-of-kitesurfing

https://www.ikointl.com/blog/complete-beginners-guide-know-everything-about-kitesurfing

About the Author

Kerri Mazzarella was raised on the East Coast of southern Florida. Living near the beach has given her the opportunity to watch all types of surfing throughout her life. All four of her children have done their fair share of bodysurfing over the years for fun! Surfing is a great way to connect with the ocean and get some exercise. Her youngest son is a competitive shortboard surfer and travels all over the world to surf!

Written by: Kerri Mazzarella
Designed by: Bobbie Houser
Series Development: James Earley
Proofreader: Janine Deschenes
Educational Consultant: Marie Lemke M.Ed.

Photographs:
t = Top, c = Center, b = Bottom, l = Left, r = Right

Alamy: ZUMA Press: p. 2 tr; Addictive Stock: p. 12 l; Martin Rickett: p. 24; jbdodane: p. 25 t

Newscom: Makenastockmedia/ZUMA Press: p. 25 b

Shutterstock: Yankovsky88: cover, p. 1, 11; Yana Mavlyutova: p. 4, 8; sainthorant: p. 5; adriaticfoto: p. 6; Protasov AN: p. 7; Wallenrock: p. 9-10, 28-29; Apustus: p. 12 br; Roxane 134: p. 13; p. 14; aerophoto: p. 15; EpicStockMedia: p. 16; Mark Medlock: p. 17; Beata Janeczko: p. 18; Luz Zuluaga Photography: p. 19; Alexander Kolomietz: p. 20; Jens Breuer: p. 21; K-FK: p. 22; mcherevan: p. 23; silvae: p. 26; PeopleImages.com - Yuri A: p. 27

Crabtree Publishing

crabtreebooks.com 800-387-7650

Printed in the U.S.A./052025/CP20250422

Published in Canada
Crabtree Publishing
616 Welland Ave.
St. Catharines, Ontario
L2M 5V6

Published in the United States
Crabtree Publishing
347 Fifth Ave
Suite 1402-145
New York, NY 10016

Library and Archives Canada Cataloguing in Publication
Available at Library and Archives Canada

Library of Congress Cataloging-in-Publication Data
Available at the Library of Congress

Hardcover: 978-1-0398-8025-2
Paperback: 978-1-0398-8385-7
Ebook (pdf): 978-1-0398-8145-7
Epub: 978-1-0398-8265-2